Breakfasts in Jars Cookbook

Healthy, Quick and Easy Mason Jar Recipes

Louise Davidson

ISBN: 978-1535432771

Printed in the United States

Avant-Propos

Breakfast might be the most important meal of the day, but it is also the meal people skip most often. Making sure to have a bite in the morning helps keep your energy up for the rest of the day, given that your body has been fasting throughout the night.

This book aims to help you to start the day right with 50 delicious and nutritious morning options. The recipes inside provide an assortment of hot and cold breakfast dishes from overnight oatmeal to cinnamon rolls. Most of them can be prepared in under 15 minutes, or even made the night before so your morning routine will be much more bearable and stress free.

One of the keys to putting together these make-ahead breakfasts is the use of canning jars. In recent years, glass containers have been gaining popularity in part due to their versatility. Not only do they make food presentation more appealing, but they are also good for food storage and reheating. Assemble the ingredients inside the jars a day before, and whenever you are ready to serve them, either eat out of the jars directly or conveniently stick them inside the microwave or oven to warm them through.

The options are endless when it comes to preparing these jar breakfasts, and don't feel stressed out about getting it right. You can alter the recipes with ingredients that best suit you and your family's preferences. I am hopeful that this book will help your early morning hours be more organized and run as smoothly as possible.

Contents

Introduction

Getting ready in the morning can be a frantic affair. In our mad scramble to get out of the house, breakfast is usually at the back of the mind for most people. Instead of reaching out for a store-bought granola bar or donut, start your day right with a homemade jar breakfast. Your body will thank you later for feeding it with healthy fuel to keep it energized for the day ahead.

Making a nutritious and delicious breakfast should not be complicated. This book aims to simplify the preparation process with 50 easy and fuss free recipes that you can be put together in less than 15 minutes, or better still, the night before. The key to doing so would be to use canning jars. These glass containers are trending all over the internet for their beautiful presentation, but in this case, they are also valued for the convenience they offer.

Most of the assembling can be done inside the jars themselves, which helps simplify the preparation process. Not only is food made inside the glass vessels, it can also be stored there, and will be ready to be cooked or consumed immediately. Heating or re-heating can be done in a cinch because the containers are microwave and oven safe.

Many of this book's recipes can be made the night before, which is a relief for mums who have many mouths to feed in the morning. Those in a morning hurry will also be able to grab and go with these jar breakfasts. You can have peace of mind knowing that the containers are sturdy and leak proof, because they were originally designed for canning purposes.

This book offers an assortment of breakfast-in-a-jar recipes that are sure to please everyone in the family. All-time breakfast favorites – fruit and granola yogurt parfaits and breakfast smoothies – are included, together with latest health food trends. Think quinoa breakfast bowl, overnight oatmeal and chia seed pudding. There are also hot options available and they can be made in the microwave or baked in the oven.

These jar breakfasts are presented in individual portion sizes, which is perfect for those who are watching their daily intake. The recipes can be easily tweaked to suit individual's dietary and personal preferences. Instead of regular milk, use almond or coconut milk if you adhere to a plant-based diet. Replace the fruits or nuts with your favorite toppings. Explore the endless opportunities and customize the ingredients to your own liking.

After finishing your meal, give the jars a quick rinse or stick them in the dishwasher. They will come out as good as new, all ready for you to pack your next breakfast inside.

Tips for Preparing Breakfast in Jars

The breakfast jar recipes in this book are supposed to be simple and easy to put together. One of the keys to ensuring that they turn out well is to be aware of how much time is needed to make these meals. While some of these recipes are suitable for putting together days in advance, others are best made on the spot. The following are some nifty tips and tricks to help make your preparation process much easier.

1. For overnight oatmeal and grain/chia pudding:
Allow oats, grains, and seeds to soak in the liquid for at least 4 hours, but preferably overnight so they can soften. When you're ready to eat, check the consistency of the oatmeal or pudding. This is because the oats, grains, and seeds tend to soak up a lot of liquid and might become quite thick when left overnight. If you prefer a thinner consistency, simply add more liquid, stir it through and adjust accordingly based on your personal preference.

Although most of the recipes in this book call for milk, swap it out with other breakfast beverages if you like, including fresh juices, soy milk or nut milk, for a fresh new take. Do check for the sweetness level of the oatmeal or pudding when using sweetened drinks.

On colder mornings, place the oatmeal in the microwave to warm it up for 1-2 minutes on high. The warm fresh fruits will be mushier in consistency as well as sweeter after heating through. Otherwise, remove the fruits before heating in the microwave, or add them afterwards. When making the chia pudding, there is a tendency for the seeds to clump together. Give the jar a good shake occasionally to disperse the seeds and help them soak up the liquid better.

2. For breakfast smoothies:
To prepare smoothies for the week ahead, portion out the ingredients needed for individual servings into separate plastic bags. Label them clearly and stick them into your freezer. This will make preparing the juices much easier throughout the week because you do not have to go scrambling around to find different ingredients and weigh out the portions.

Another good trick is to use a standard-size, narrow-mouth canning jar (not wide-mouth jars) as an accessory for the blender. Place all the ingredients into a standard jar and screw the blender base with the blade on top of the jar securely. Fit into the blender and it will work perfectly. Once all the ingredients are smooth and creamy, drink straight from the jar!

3. For microwave meals:
Each microwave model is different, depending on the make and wattage of the machine. Cooking time might also vary based on the thickness of the jar that you are using. It is best to be conservative when estimating cooking time to avoid overcooking. If the food is not cooked through after the recommended timing, place it back in the microwave and cook in 30 second intervals until it is done. You might need to experiment with your microwave to find out its optimal cooking timing. Most importantly, always remove the jar lids when cooking in microwaves because the metal lids will catch fire and ruin your machine.

4. For baking:

There have been safety concerns on the internet regarding the use of canning jars inside the oven. These glass containers were originally designed to withstand high temperatures inside hot water baths and pressure cookers. As such, they are likely to be safe to use in your oven. Furthermore, many online food bloggers say they've baked with their jars hundreds of times, and they have never experienced breakage before.

But for your peace of mind, the following are some safety measures to undertake to minimize any risk.

1. When baking, unscrew the jar lids to prevent undue pressure from building up inside a covered jar.
2. Bake in a cold oven. This will give the jars enough time to warm up as the oven is preheating, to avoid sudden temperature shocks that might result in glass breakage.
3. If you are taking jars out of the freezer or fridge, let them sit in room temperature for at least 30 minutes to an hour before placing them inside the cold oven. This step also helps prevent sudden temperature changes for the glass.

When taking the hot jars out of the oven, take extra care when handling them because the glass is very hot and will result in severe burns if you were to accidentally touch them. Set the jars aside for at least 10-15 minutes to cool down before digging into your meals.

Types of Jars to Use

There is a wide assortment of canning jars available in the market – many different sizes and designs. One of the first differences you might notice is that there are wide- and narrow-mouth varieties. Narrow-mouth jars, or sometimes called standard size jars, are vessels with mouths that are smaller than the bodies and they typically feature rounded shoulders. They can be mounted on most blenders, so use them for preparing, storing, and transporting your drinks. The wide-mouth variety is suitable for storing bulky food because it is much easier to get items in or out of the jar. Use these for baking as well because they allow the food to rise more evenly when compared to their narrow mouth counterparts.

As for jar sizes, these depend on individual portion sizes. For breakfast, half-pint (8 ounce or 1 cup) and pint-sized (16 ounce or 2 cup) jars are usually used. However, you can easily increase or decrease the jar size based on your dietary restrictions. Also, use these jar sizes to help you track your daily intake.

When choosing jar lids, take into consideration the cooking method. Jars that come with attached rubber lids are best used for refrigerator only meals since they should not be placed in the microwave or oven. Others come with detachable metal lids that are traditionally used for sealing the jar during the canning process. These have a mouth lid and a band to ensure a tight fit. Always remove the lids when using these inside the microwave or oven.

Plastic storage caps are also becoming popular options. Fitting snugly on top of most canning jars, they are more convenient than metal lids because they are one piece, thereby reducing the risk of losing the band or the metal lid. But these plastic caps are neither heat safe nor vacuum sealed.

Recipes

Goji Berries and Cacao Nibs Overnight Oats

Servings: 1

Ingredients
⅔ cup rolled oats
1 teaspoon chia seeds
¼ cup almond milk
1 teaspoon raw honey
1 tablespoon goji berries
2 teaspoons cacao nibs
1 teaspoon hemp seed

Preparation
1. In a pint-sized jar, soak the oats and chia seeds in the almond milk overnight in the refrigerator
2. When ready to consume, mix the honey thoroughly with the oats. Top it off with the goji berries, cacao nibs, and hemp seed.
3. Eat it cold or warm it up in the microwave.

Nutritional Facts (196 g per single serving)
Calories 526
Fats 13 g
Carbs 85 g
Protein 21 g
Sodium 68 mg

Pomegranate and Almond Overnight Oats

Servings: 1

Ingredients
⅓ cup muesli mix, or plain oats
¼ teaspoon cinnamon
1 teaspoon brown sugar
2 teaspoons chia seeds
¼ cup milk
¼ cup plain yogurt
2 tablespoons pomegranate seeds
5 toasted almonds, roughly chopped

Preparation
1. In a pint-sized jar, stir the muesli, cinnamon, and brown sugar together until well combined.
2. Add the chia seeds, milk, yogurt, pomegranate seeds, and chopped almonds. Cover with a lid and refrigerate overnight.
3. Serve the next day, cold or warmed in the microwave.

Nutritional Facts (191 g per single serving)
Calories 293
Fats 11 g
Carbs 12 g
Protein 38 g
Sodium 57 mg

Pumpkin Spice Overnight Oats

Servings: 1

Ingredients
½ cup almond milk
½ cup rolled oats
1 tablespoon pumpkin puree
1 teaspoon vanilla extract
1 teaspoon pumpkin pie spice
Pumpkin seeds, for garnish

Preparation
1. Combine the milk, oats, pumpkin puree, vanilla extract, and spices in a pint-sized jar. Refrigerate it overnight.
2. Serve the next day straight out of the fridge and finish it with crunchy pumpkin seeds.

Nutritional Facts (234 g per single serving)
Calories 331
Fats 6 g
Carbs 55 g
Protein 14 g
Sodium 154 mg

Chocolate Peanut Butter Oatmeal

Servings: 1

Ingredients
½ cup oats
1 teaspoon chia seeds
½ cup unsweetened soy milk
1 teaspoon maple syrup
1 tablespoon peanut butter
1 teaspoon raw peanuts
1 tablespoon dark chocolate chips

Preparation
1. Place the oats, chia seeds, soy milk, maple syrup, and peanut butter in a pint-sized jar. Give it a good mix before refrigerating it overnight.
2. The next day, add the peanuts and dark chocolate chips on top before enjoying it cold.

Nutritional Facts (239 g per single serving)
Calories 546
Fats 18 g
Carbs 74 g
Protein 22 g
Sodium 170 mg

Black Forest Oatmeal

Servings: 1

Ingredients
½ cup frozen cherries
1 tablespoon cocoa powder
2 teaspoons maple syrup
½ teaspoon vanilla extract
½ cup almond milk
½ cup Greek yogurt
½ cup rolled oats
1 tablespoon unsweetened shredded coconut
1 tablespoon dark chocolate chips

Preparation
1. In a blender, puree the cherries, cocoa powder, maple syrup, vanilla extract, and almond milk. Pour into a pint-sized jar.
2. Stir the yogurt and oats into the puree and mix thoroughly. Cover the jar with a lid and refrigerate overnight.
3. The next day, mix in half the shredded coconut and chocolate chips. If the oatmeal is too thick, thin it with more milk or yogurt. Top it off with the rest of the coconut and chocolate chips before eating.

Nutritional Facts (451 g per single serving)
Calories 670
Fats 26 g
Carbs 84 g
Protein 27 g
Sodium 148 mg

Mocha Overnight Oats

Servings: 1

Ingredients
½ cup almond milk
½ cup brewed coffee, cooled to room temperature
2 tablespoons cacao powder
½ cup rolled oats
1 tablespoon maple syrup
1 tablespoon unsweetened shredded coconut

Preparation
1. Place the almond milk, coffee, cacao powder, oats, and maple syrup in a pint-sized jar. Mix well, cover the jar with a lid, and refrigerate overnight
2. To consume, top it with shredded coconut before devouring.

Nutritional Facts (376 g per single serving)
Calories 511
Fats 19 g
Carbs 75 g
Protein 17 g
Sodium 108 mg

Tropical Mango Coconut Overnight Oats

Servings: 1

Ingredients
½ cup rolled oats
½ cup unsweetened almond milk
½ cup mango, diced
1 tablespoon unsweetened shredded coconut
1 tablespoon agave nectar

Preparation
1. In a pint-sized jar, combine all the ingredients and give it a good mix. Cover the jar with a lid and refrigerate overnight.
2. Serve the next day straight out of the fridge

Nutritional Facts (330 g per single serving)
Calories 549
Fats 17 g
Carbs 85 g
Protein 16 g
Sodium 103 mg

Banana and Almond Oatmeal

Servings: 1

Ingredients
¼ cup rolled oats
1 tablespoon chia seeds
1 teaspoon cinnamon
¾ cup unsweetened almond milk
½ ripe banana, sliced
1 tablespoon natural almond butter
1 teaspoon maple syrup

Preparation
1. Soak the oats, chia seeds, and cinnamon in the almond milk, in a pint-sized jar, overnight in the fridge.
2. To serve, microwave the banana and almond butter in the microwave on high power for a minute. Add them to the oats.
3. Finish with the maple syrup and enjoy.

Nutritional Facts (337 g per single serving)
Calories 407
Fats 17 g
Carbs 53 g
Protein 14 g
Sodium 146 mg

Chocolate Dates Overnight Oats

Servings: 1

Ingredients
½ cup rolled oats
½ cup unsweetened almond milk
1 Medjool date, pitted and finely chopped
½ tablespoon unsweetened cocoa powder
¼ teaspoon vanilla extract
1 teaspoon maple syrup
2 teaspoons pecans, chopped

Preparation
1. In a pint-sized jar, combine the oats, milk, date, cocoa powder, and vanilla extract until well mixed. Place in the refrigerator overnight.
2. When ready to consume, stir in the maple syrup and finish it off with chopped pecans.

Nutritional Facts (248 g per single serving)
Calories 450
Fats 11 g
Carbs 78 g
Protein 16 g
Sodium 97 mg

Banana Chia Pudding

Servings: 1

Ingredients
2 ripe bananas
¼ cup coconut milk
1 teaspoon vanilla extract
¾ teaspoon ground cinnamon
2 tablespoons chia seeds
1 teaspoon unsweetened shredded coconut

Preparation
1. In a blender, puree one banana, coconut milk, vanilla extract, and cinnamon. Pour it into a pint-sized jar.
2. Add the chia seeds to the jar, mix, and refrigerate overnight. Take the jar out occasionally and give it a good stir.
3. To serve, slice up another banana and top it off with shredded coconut.

Nutritional Facts (322 g per single serving)
Calories 366
Fats 12 g
Carbs 65 g
Protein 7 g
Sodium 19 mg

Mango Lime Chia Pudding

Servings: 4

Ingredients
1 (16 ounce) can coconut milk
3 cups frozen mango chunks
¼ cup maple syrup
1 tablespoon lime zest
¼ cup lime juice
⅓ cup chia seeds
¼ cup hemp seeds
4 cups fresh mango, pineapple, banana, or your desired fruit topping

Preparation
1. Puree the coconut milk, frozen mango, maple syrup, lime zest, and lime juice in a blender until it becomes smooth. Pour the mixture into 4 pint-sized jars.
2. Divide the chia and hemp seeds among the jars, and stir well.
3. Refrigerate the pudding overnight.
4. When ready to serve, finish each jar off with a cup of fresh fruit.

Nutritional Facts (459 g per single serving)
Calories 580
Fats 34 g
Carbs 70 g
Protein 10 g
Sodium 23 mg

Warm Apple Cinnamon Chia Pudding

Servings: 2

Ingredients
2 cups unsweetened almond milk
1 teaspoon vanilla extract
1 cup chia seeds
2 tablespoons unsweetened shredded coconut flakes
2 apples, cored and chopped
2 teaspoons cinnamon
For garnish: shredded coconut, apple cubes, cinnamon

Preparation
1. In two half-pint canning jars, pour the almond milk and vanilla extract. Heat them in the microwave for 2 minutes, until warm.
2. Pour the chia seeds in and stir constantly for about 2 minutes. Set the mixture aside for 5 minutes so the chia seeds can soften.
3. Garnish with the shredded coconut, apple cubes, and/or cinnamon.

Nutritional Facts (517 g per single serving)
Calories 768
Fats 49 g
Carbs 71 g
Protein 22 g
Sodium 212 mg

Triple Berry Chia Pudding

Servings: 2

Ingredients
1 cup unsweetened almond milk
¾ cup fresh blueberries, blackberries, and raspberries
2 tablespoons chia seeds
1 teaspoon honey

Preparation
1. Divide the almond milk, fruit, chia seeds, and honey between 2 pint-sized jars. Cover with lids and give them a good shake. Place them in the refrigerator for 15 minutes.
2. Take the jars out of the fridge and give them another good shake. Return back to fridge and let them sit overnight.
3. Enjoy the pudding chilled the next morning.

Nutritional Facts (197 g per single serving)
Calories 107
Fats 4 g
Carbs 14 g
Protein 4 g
Sodium 95 mg

Creamy Chocolate Chia Pudding

Servings: 4

Ingredients
1 ½ cups unsweetened almond milk
⅓ cup chia seeds
¼ cup unsweetened cocoa powder
4 tablespoons maple syrup
½ teaspoon ground cinnamon
¼ teaspoon sea salt
For topping: Fresh fruit slices, granola or shredded coconut

Preparation
1. In a large mixing bowl, combine all the ingredients and give them a good stir.
2. Divide the mixture among 4 pint-sized jars. Cover with lids and refrigerate overnight.
3. Serve them the next day, chilled, with your desired topping.

Nutritional Facts (164 g per single serving)
Calories 275
Fats 14 g
Carbs 34 g
Protein 8 g
Sodium 80 mg

Raspberry Vanilla Chia Pudding

Servings: 2

Ingredients
1 cup vanilla soy milk
4 tablespoons chia seeds
1 cup raspberries + extra for garnish
2 teaspoons vanilla extract

Preparation
1. Divide the ingredients equally between 2 pint-sized jars. Cover with lids and give them a good shake.
2. Place them in the refrigerator overnight.
3. Serve them the next day with more fresh raspberries.

Nutritional Facts (204 g per single serving)
Calories 188
Fats 9 g
Carbs 22 g
Protein 7 g
Sodium 72 mg

Overnight Buckwheat Chia Pudding

Servings: 1

Ingredients
½ cup raw buckwheat groats
¾ cup almond milk
2 tablespoons chia seeds
1 tablespoon maple syrup
1 teaspoon ground cinnamon
¼ teaspoon vanilla extract
1 banana, diced

Preparation
1. Soak the buckwheat in 1 cup of water overnight. When ready to use, drain and rinse it.
2. In a medium bowl, mix the buckwheat, almond milk, chia seeds, maple syrup, cinnamon, and vanilla extract until thoroughly combined.
3. Transfer the pudding into a pint-sized jar. Cover with a lid and set it aside for at least 15 minutes for the chia seeds to plump up.
4. Top it off with bananas and you are ready to dig in.

Nutritional Facts (438 g per single serving)
Calories 569
Fats 10 g
Carbs 110 g
Protein 16 g
Sodium 157 mg

Buckwheat Cashew Parfait

Servings: 4

Ingredients
1 cup buckwheat groats (soaked in water overnight)
½ cup raw cashews (soaked in water overnight)
1 pint raspberries
1 medium pear, peeled and diced
1 tablespoon chia seeds
½ teaspoon vanilla extract
½ ripe banana
½ cup almond milk
¼ teaspoon sea salt

Preparation
1. Soak the buckwheat and cashews in water overnight.
2. When you're ready to prepare the jars, make the fruit compote. In a small saucepan, cook the raspberries and pear over medium heat until the fruits become soft and mushy. Mix in the chia seeds. Set the saucepan aside for the chia seeds to plump up.
3. Drain and rinse the soaked buckwheat and cashews. Place them in a blender, together with the vanilla extract, banana, almond milk and sea salt. Puree them until it becomes smooth
4. To assemble, prepare 4 pint-sized jars. Place half the cashew puree at the bottom of the jars. Next, add the fruit compote, followed by the rest of the cashew puree.
5. Dig in immediately, or cover with lids and keep them in the fridge for up to 4 days.

Nutritional Facts (244 g per single serving)
Calories 397
Fats 15 g
Carbs 61 g
Protein 12 g
Sodium 33 mg

Coconut Quinoa with Cherry Compote

Servings: 4

Ingredients
1 cup quinoa
1 cup almond milk
1 (16 ounce) can light coconut milk
1 pound frozen, pitted cherries
2 tablespoons water
Pinch salt
1 tablespoon maple syrup
½ cup almonds, roughly chopped
½ cup unsweetened shredded coconut

Preparation
1. In a medium saucepan, cook the quinoa in the almond milk on medium heat until all the liquid is absorbed. Next, slowly pour the coconut milk into the pot, stirring constantly, until most of the liquid is absorbed, but it should still be creamy and moist. Cover with a lid and set it aside.
2. In a small saucepan, cook the cherries, water, and a pinch of salt over low or medium-low heat for about 10-15 minutes, to allow the cherries to release their juices. Once the sauce has thickened, stir in the maple syrup and cook for another 2 minutes. Remove from the heat.
3. To assemble, put a layer of quinoa in the bottom of 4 pint-sized jars, followed by the cherries, almonds, and shredded coconut. Enjoy them warm or cover with lids and refrigerate them for up to 4 days.

Nutritional Facts (381 g per single serving)

Calories 605

Fats 38 g

Carbs 55 g

Protein 14 g

Sodium 86 mg

Egg and Fruits Breakfast Quinoa

Servings: 2

Ingredients
1 large egg
2 egg whites
1 tablespoon milk
Pinch sea salt
3 cups cooked quinoa
2 cups pomegranate and blueberries, or any fruits of your choice

Preparation
1. In a small bowl, whisk together the egg, egg whites, milk, and sea salt.
2. Heat a small skillet over medium heat. Pour in the egg mixture and scramble it.
3. Spoon 2 tablespoons of the egg into each of the 2 pint-sized jars. Add a layer of quinoa, followed by more eggs, quinoa, pomegranate, eggs, and finish off with the blueberries.
4. Enjoy it warm or cold.

Nutritional Facts (504 g per single serving)
Calories 505
Fats 9 g
Carbs 87 g
Protein 21 g
Sodium 116 mg

Apples and Goat Cheese Overnight Bulgur Bowl

Servings: 4

Ingredients

1 cup bulgur wheat
1 ½ cups low-fat milk
2 tablespoons almond butter
¼ teaspoon ground cinnamon
1 cup apple, peeled and chopped
¼ cup plain, reduced-fat Greek yogurt
2 ounces goat cheese, crumbled
2 tablespoons thinly sliced almonds, toasted
2 teaspoons honey

Preparation

1. Soak the bulgur overnight in the milk.
2. In a medium bowl, mix the bulgur, almond butter, and cinnamon together. Add the apple, yogurt, and goat cheese and combine well.
3. Divide the bulgur equally among 4 pint-sized jars.
4. Finish with the almond slices and a drizzle of honey on top.

Nutritional Facts (220 g per single serving)

Calories 342
Fats 13 g
Carbs 42 g
Protein 17 g
Sodium 131 mg

Peach Yogurt Parfait

Servings: 4

Ingredients

2 ripe peaches, peeled, pitted and diced
¼ teaspoon ground cinnamon
3 tablespoons honey, divided
2 cups Greek yogurt
½ cup granola
Toppings: fruits of your choice

Preparation

1. In a medium bowl, coat the peaches with cinnamon and 1 tablespoon of honey. Set them aside.
2. In a small bowl, combine the yogurt with the rest of the honey.
3. Scoop a layer of yogurt into the bottom of each of 4 pint-sized jars. Next, add a layer of peaches, followed by granola. Repeat the layers again until the jars are filled. Finish them off with more fruits of your choice.

Nutritional Facts (236 g per single serving)

Calories 277
Fats 11 g
Carbs 34 g
Protein 15 g
Sodium 50 mg

Flaxseed Raspberry Yogurt

Servings: 2

Ingredients
½ cup yogurt
½ cup flaxseed meal
⅓ cup unsweetened almond milk
3 tablespoons vanilla protein powder
3 tablespoons honey
¾ cup raspberries

Preparation
1. Divide the ingredients between two pint-sized jars. Give the mixture a good stir.
2. Cover them with lids and place them in the fridge overnight.

Nutritional Facts (221 g per single serving)
Calories 354
Fats 14 g
Carbs 42 g
Protein 20 g
Sodium 80 mg

Blueberry Apple Yogurt Parfait

Servings: 2

Ingredients
2 ½ cups vanilla yogurt
1 ¼ cups granola

To make the sauce:
2 apples, cored and slices
½ cup blueberries
1 tablespoon lemon juice
1 teaspoon vanilla extract

Preparation
1. To make the apple blueberry sauce: Place all the ingredients in a small saucepan and bring the mixture to boil over medium heat. Once boiled, reduce the heat to low and allow the mixture to simmer for about 20-30 minutes, or until the apple becomes very soft.
2. Allow the mixture to cool before whizzing it up with an immersion blender.
3. To make the parfait, take two pint-sized canning jars and layer them with vanilla yogurt, granola, and the sauce.
4. Let it set inside the refrigerator for at least an hour before consuming it.

Nutritional Facts (529 g per single serving)
Calories 690
Fats 19 g
Carbs 114 g
Protein 21 g
Sodium 166 mg

Strawberry and Chocolate Yogurt Parfait

Servings: 1

Ingredients
¾ cup Greek plain yogurt
⅔ cup granola
6 strawberries, cut in quarters
1 ounce dark chocolate, cut in small chunks

Preparation
1. In a pint-sized jar, layer a few tablespoons of yogurt, followed by half the granola, a few strawberry slices, and a few chocolate pieces.
2. Repeat the layers until the jar is filled completely.
3. Finish with a dollop of yogurt and more strawberry slices.

Nutritional Facts (411 g per single serving)
Calories 791
Fats 42 g
Carbs 73 g
Protein 31 g
Sodium 96 mg

Banana Split Yogurt Parfait

Servings: 1

Ingredients
1 small banana, sliced
1 cup frozen strawberries, sliced
½ cup vanilla Greek yogurt
1 tablespoon chocolate chips

Preparation
1. Place a few slices of banana in the bottom of a pint-sized jar. Next, scoop a layer of yogurt, followed by more bananas, strawberries, and chocolate chips.
2. Repeat the layers until the jar is filled. Cover with a lid and refrigerate for up to 2 days.

Nutritional Facts (252 g per single serving)
Calories 288
Fats 7 g
Carbs 13 g
Protein 44 g
Sodium 64 mg

Blackberry Pie Parfait

Servings: 1

Ingredients
6 ounces blackberry yogurt
¼ cup rolled oats
½ cup fresh blackberries
½ cup graham cracker crumbs

Preparation
1. In a small bowl, combine the oats with the yogurt.
2. Place a layer of the yogurt mixture in the bottom of a pint-sized jar. Layer half of the blackberries on top of the yogurt, followed by the graham cracker crumbs. Add the rest of the yogurt and finish with the remaining blackberries.

Nutritional Facts (319 g per single serving)
Calories 587
Fats 18 g
Carbs 90 g
Protein 19 g
Sodium 402 mg

Coconut Pineapple Breakfast Parfait

Servings: 1

Ingredients
6 ounces coconut yogurt
¼ cup rolled oats
½ cup fresh pineapple, diced
½ cup toasted shredded coconut

Preparation
1. Mix together oats and yogurt in a small bowl.
2. Scoop 3-4 tablespoons of the yogurt mixture into a pint-sized jar. Layer 2-3 tablespoons of the pineapple, followed by 3 tablespoons of shredded coconut. Repeat the layers until the jar is completely filled.

Nutritional Facts (349 g per single serving)
Calories 827
Fats 53 g
Carbs 77 g
Protein 19 g
Sodium 113 mg

Summer Berries Granola Yogurt

Servings: 5

Ingredients
1 ¼ cups frozen mixed berries
5 teaspoons honey
1 ¼ cups vanilla Greek yogurt
5 tablespoons granola

Preparation
1. Divide the berries among five half-pint jelly jars
2. Drizzle the honey over the fruit.
3. Portion the yogurt equally among the jars, and finish with a generous scattering of granola.

Nutritional Facts (116 g per single serving)
Calories 137
Fats 8 g
Carbs 63 g
Protein 17 g
Sodium 28 mg

Pumpkin Spice Granola Parfait

Servings: 1

Ingredients
½ cup vanilla yogurt
1 teaspoon chia seeds
1 tablespoon pure pumpkin puree
½ teaspoon pumpkin pie spice
6 tablespoons granola

Preparation
1. In a small bowl, mix the yogurt, chia seeds, pumpkin pie spice, and pumpkin puree together.
2. Transfer half the mixture into a half-pint jar.
3. Scoop 3 tablespoons of granola into the jar. Add the rest of the yogurt mixture.
4. Finish the jar with the remaining granola.

Nutritional Facts (208 g per single serving)
Calories 415
Fats 17 g
Carbs 46 g
Protein 20 g
Sodium 68 mg

Chocolate Banana Almond Smoothie

Servings: 2

Ingredients
1 cup unsweetened almond milk
2 tablespoons almond butter
2 tablespoons unsweetened cocoa powder
½ banana
1 teaspoon vanilla extract
2 cups ice

Preparation
1. In a blender, mix all the ingredients together until smooth.
2. Pour the smoothie into 2 pint-sized jars to serve.

Nutritional Facts (404 g per single serving)
Calories 161
Fats 11 g
Carbs 15 g
Protein 6 g
Sodium 99 mg

Homemade Maple Walnut Granola Parfait

Servings: 4

Ingredients
For granola:
¾ cup rolled oats
¼ cup hemp seeds
⅓ cup walnuts, chopped
1 teaspoon cinnamon
½ teaspoon salt
1 tablespoon coconut oil, melted
3 tablespoons maple syrup
¼ cup coconut flakes

For parfaits:
2 cups frozen mixed berries
2 cups plain yogurt
4 teaspoons maple syrup

Preparation
1. Preheat the oven to 300°F. Prepare a 13x9 baking sheet lined with parchment paper.
2. In a medium mixing bowl, stir the rolled oats, hemp seeds, walnuts, cinnamon, and salt together. Pour in the coconut oil and maple syrup, and toss to combine.
3. Transfer the mixture to the prepared baking sheet. Bake for 20 minutes.

4. Remove the granola from the oven and mix in the coconut flakes. Give everything a good mix and continue to bake for another 15 minutes. Remove the granola from the oven and allow it to cool down for 15 minutes before assembling the parfaits.
5. Place half a cup of frozen berries into 4 half-pint jars. Drizzle the maple syrup over the berries. Divide the yogurt among the jars and top them off with the granola.

Nutritional Facts (288 g per single serving)
Calories 574
Fats 32 g
Carbs 53 g
Protein 24 g
Sodium 55 mg

Dairy-free Apple Cinnamon Smoothie

Servings: 1

Ingredients
1 cup coconut water
4 raw almonds
1 teaspoon vanilla extract
1 teaspoon ground cinnamon
1 medium apple, cored
½ scoop unsweetened protein powder
1 tablespoon ground flaxseed

Preparation
1. Blend all the ingredients in a blender until smooth.
2. Pour the smoothie into a pint-sized jar to serve.

Nutritional Facts (448 g per single serving)
Calories 257
Fats 5 g
Carbs 41 g
Protein 12 g
Sodium 309 mg

Pineapple and Blueberry Smoothie

Servings: 1

Ingredients
⅓ cup vanilla non-fat Greek yogurt
1 tablespoon almond butter
½ cup frozen blueberries
½ cup frozen pineapple
1 cup kale
¾ cup water

Preparation
1. In a food processor, whizz together all the ingredients until smooth and creamy.
2. Serve the smoothie immediately in a pint-sized jar.

Nutritional Facts (428 g per single serving)
Calories 326
Fats 9 g
Carbs 49 g
Protein 14 g
Sodium 100 mg

Avocado Spinach and Grape Smoothie

Servings: 1

Ingredients
2 cups spinach, packed
1 ripe pear, peeled, cored, and chopped
15 green grapes
6 ounces fat-free plain Greek yogurt
2 tablespoons avocado, roughly diced
1 tablespoons fresh lime juice

Preparation
1. In a blender, whizz together all the ingredients until smooth and creamy.
2. Serve chilled in a pint-sized jar.

Nutritional Facts (553 g per single serving)
Calories 330
Fats 6 g
Carbs 54 g
Protein 22 g
Sodium 114 mg

Blackberry Almond Breakfast Smoothie

Servings: 1

Ingredients
1 cup unsweetened almond milk
1 scoop chocolate protein powder
1 banana
1 ½ cups blackberries

Preparation
1. Blend the ingredients in a blender or food processor until the mixture reaches the desired consistency.
2. Pour into a pint-sized jar. Best enjoyed when chilled.

Nutritional Facts (643 g per single serving)
Calories 357
Fats 3 g
Carbs 62 g
Protein 24 g
Sodium 296 mg

Bacon and Eggs in a Jar

Servings: 1

Ingredients
2 eggs
1 cup spinach
¼ cup shredded mozzarella
2 slices turkey bacon
Salt and pepper, to taste

Preparation
1. In a small bowl, whisk together the eggs, cheese, and spinach. Season the mixture with salt and pepper.
2. Transfer the egg mixture into a pint-sized jar. Place it in the microwave and cook it on high for about 2 minutes. Remove it from the microwave.
3. Line a plate with 3-4 sheets of paper towel. Place the bacon on top of the paper towels and cover it with 2 more sheets. The paper towels will ensure that grease does not splatter all over the microwave. Cook the bacon on high for 1 minute. If the bacon is not cooked through, microwave in 30-second intervals until done.
4. Crumble the bacon slices on top of the eggs. Best consumed warm.

Nutritional Facts (188 g per single serving)
Calories 310
Fats 22 g
Carbs 4 g
Protein 24 g
Sodium 612 mg

Microwave Blueberry Pancakes

Servings: 4

Ingredients
1 cup flour
1 tablespoon baking powder
2 tablespoons sugar
2 tablespoons butter, melted
¾ cup milk
1 cup blueberries

Preparation
1. In a medium bowl, whisk together the flour, baking powder, and sugar.
2. Pour in the melted butter and milk, and stir to combine.
3. Spoon 2-3 tablespoons of blueberries into the bottom of 4 half-pint jars. Pour the pancake batter into the jar up to the halfway mark.
4. Microwave the jars for about 1 minute, or until a toothpick comes out clean. If uncooked, put it back into the microwave to cook for another 20 seconds.
5. Serve with your favorite toppings, including maple syrup, butter or more blueberries.

Nutritional Facts (112 g per single serving)
Calories 183
Fats 8 g
Carbs 26 g
Protein 3 g
Sodium 24 mg

Breakfast Bread Pudding

Servings: 6

Ingredients

1 cup whole grain oat flour
½ cup whole grain barley flour
½ cup whole grain brown rice flour
2 tablespoons ground chia seeds
2 teaspoons baking powder
½ teaspoon baking soda
1 teaspoon cinnamon
½ teaspoon salt
1 cup low-fat buttermilk
½ cup water
2 teaspoons vanilla extract
⅓ cup honey
3 cups low-fat vanilla yogurt
3 cups ripe berries

Preparation

1. In a large mixing bowl, whisk together the flours, chia seeds, baking powder, baking soda, cinnamon, and salt.
2. In a separate bowl, stir together the buttermilk, water, vanilla extract, and honey. Incorporate the wet ingredients into the dry ingredients until just mixed.
3. Pour the batter into 6 pint-sized jars. Cover with lids and let it rest in the refrigerator for at least 30 minutes, or up until 5 days until you are ready to cook.

4. Place a jar into the microwave and cook on high for about 1 minute. To check if it is cooked through, stick a toothpick in and it should come out clean. Otherwise, place it back in the microwave again and cook in 20-second intervals until done.
5. Top each jar off with ½ cup each of yogurt and berries.

Nutritional Facts (322 g per single serving)
Calories 409
Fats 7 g
Carbs 72 g
Protein 18 g
Sodium 134 mg

Gluten-free Apple Breakfast Muffin

Servings: 1

Ingredients
1 tablespoon butter
2 tablespoons unsweetened applesauce
1 egg
¼ teaspoon vanilla extract
1 teaspoon maple syrup
3 tablespoons almond flour
½ teaspoon cinnamon
⅛ teaspoon baking powder
Pinch of salt
1 tablespoon apple, peeled, cored and finely diced
1 teaspoon walnuts, roughly chopped
1 teaspoon cold butter

Preparation
1. Put the first tablespoon of butter in a half-pint jar, and melt it in the microwave.
2. Stir in the applesauce, egg, vanilla extract, and maple syrup.
3. Incorporate the flour, cinnamon, baking powder, and salt until just combined.
4. Crumble in the apple, walnuts, and cold butter.
5. Microwave on high for about 1 minute. To check for doneness, stick a toothpick into the muffin and it should come out clean. Otherwise, microwave it again in 20-second intervals until it is cooked through.
6. Serve immediately.

Nutritional Facts (148 g per single serving)
Calories 388
Fats 34 g
Carbs 14 g
Protein 12 g
Sodium 76 mg

No-fuss Crustless Quiche

Servings: 1

Ingredients
1 large egg
1 ½ tablespoons whole milk
1 teaspoon butter
4 grape tomatoes, halved
2 tablespoons fresh bread, torn
1 tablespoon grated cheese
1 teaspoon chopped fresh herbs
Salt and pepper, to taste

Preparation
1. Melt the butter in a half-pint jar in the microwave.
2. Whisk in the egg, milk, salt, and pepper until all the ingredients are thoroughly combined.
3. Gently drop the tomatoes, bread, and cheese into the jar. Avoid stirring it too much. Scatter the herbs on top of mixture.
4. Microwave on high for about a minute, or until the eggs are cooked through.
5. Best served immediately.

Nutritional Facts (183 g per single serving)
Calories 221
Fats 11 g
Carbs 18 g
Protein 14 g
Sodium 296 mg

Sweet Potato Hash

Servings: 1

Ingredients
1 small sweet potato (about 1 cup)
2 tablespoons green pepper, chopped
1 tablespoon red onion, chopped
2 tablespoons grated cheese
Pinch of salt and pepper
2 teaspoons rosemary
¼ tablespoons butter

Preparation
1. Peel and dice the sweet potato into small chunks. Place the pieces into a pint-sized jar. Cover the jar with plastic wrap.
2. Microwave for about 3-4 minutes, or until the pieces are soft and tender.
3. Add the rest of the ingredients, and give everything a good mix.
4. Put the jar back into the microwave and cook for another 40 seconds to 1 minute, so the cheese melts.
5. Enjoy your breakfast!

Nutritional Facts (400 g per single serving)
Calories 241
Fats 4 g
Carbs 41 g
Protein 10 g
Sodium 216 mg

Peanut Butter Breakfast Cookie

Servings: 1

Ingredients
½ medium ripe banana
1 ½ tablespoons peanut butter
½ tablespoon honey
1 tablespoon milk
4 tablespoons rolled oats
1 tablespoon raisins

Preparation
1. Using a fork, mash the banana in a half-pint jar.
2. Add the peanut butter, honey, and milk, and give it a good stir.
3. Mix in the oats and raisins.
4. Microwave the jar for 45 seconds to 1 minute, or until the cookie becomes firm on top.
5. Best served immediately.

Nutritional Facts (169 g per single serving)
Calories 448
Fats 15 g
Carbs 69 g
Protein 15 g
Sodium 59 mg

Spinach, Ham, and Egg White Omelette

Servings: 1

Ingredients
4 egg whites
2 tablespoons cooked ham
2 tablespoons fresh baby spinach, roughly torn
1 tablespoon green pepper, diced
1 tablespoon red pepper, diced
1 tablespoon tomato, diced
1 tablespoon reduced-fat cheddar cheese
Salt and pepper, to taste

Preparation
1. Pour the egg whites into a pint-sized jar and give it a good whisk with a fork.
2. Stir in the rest of the ingredients.
3. Microwave the jar for a 1 minute and check whether the eggs are cooked. If not, cook it in 30 second intervals, until it is completely set.
4. Best served immediately.

Nutritional Facts (212 g per single serving)
Calories 180
Fats 8 g
Carbs 22 g
Protein 3 g
Sodium 717 mg

Microwave Fruit and Nut and Granola

Servings: 1

Ingredients
1 tablespoon maple syrup
2 teaspoons water
2 teaspoons vegetable oil
⅛ teaspoon fine sea salt
⅓ cup rolled oats
1 tablespoon chopped nuts (I used almond)
1 tablespoon chopped dried fruit (I used cranberries)

Preparation
1. Combine the maple syrup, water, oil, salt, oats, and nuts in a pint-sized jar.
2. Place the jar in a microwave and cook it on medium for 2 minutes. Take the jar out and give the ingredients a good stir through. Microwave it on medium for another 2 minutes, or until the oats turn golden brown.
3. Mix in the cranberries.
4. Let it rest for 5 minutes before digging in.

Nutritional Facts (109 g per single serving)
Calories 402
Fats 16 g
Carbs 56 g
Protein 10 g
Sodium 5 mg

Vegan Banana Bread in a Jar

Servings: 1

Ingredients
2 tablespoons coconut flour
¼ teaspoon baking powder
2 teaspoons brown sugar
¼ cup almond milk
½ ripe banana, mashed
1 tablespoon almond butter

Preparation
1. Mix together coconut flour and baking powder in a pint-sized jar.
2. Add the milk, sugar, banana, and almond butter until all the ingredients are just combined.
3. Place the jar in the microwave and cook it on high for 2-3 minutes, or until a toothpick comes out clean.
4. Enjoy it immediately.

Nutritional Facts (184 g per single serving)
Calories 315
Fats 14 g
Carbs 43 g
Protein 14 g
Sodium 107 mg

Blueberry French Toast

Servings: 2

Ingredients
3 slices white bread, cubed
2 eggs
1 ½ cups milk
1 tablespoon vanilla extract
1 tablespoon ground cinnamon
¼ cup granulated sugar
1 cup blueberries
2 tablespoons melted butter
¼ cup maple syrup

Preparation
1. The night before, fill 2 pint-sized jars with the bread cubes.
2. In a small bowl, whisk together the eggs, milk, vanilla extract, cinnamon, sugar, blueberries, butter, and maple syrup.
3. Pour equal amounts of the egg mixture into the 2 jars. Cover the jars with lids and place them into the refrigerator overnight to allow the bread to soak in the egg mixture.
4. Preheat the oven to 375°F. Meanwhile, take the jars out of the fridge and bring them up to room temperature.
5. Remove the lid before placing the jars in the oven. Bake for 45 minutes, or until the top turns golden brown.
6. Serve warm with more maple syrup.

Nutritional Facts (280 g per single serving)

Calories 526

Fats 18 g

Carbs 83 g

Protein 14 g

Sodium 303 mg

Breakfast Sausage and Sweet Potato Casserole

Servings: 2

Ingredients

1 bacon strip, diced
2 Italian sausage links, casings removed
6 eggs, beaten
¼ cup milk
½ teaspoon nutmeg
Salt and pepper, to taste
1 small sweet potato, peeled and shredded
1 small onion, shredded
Non-stick cooking spray

Preparation

1. Preheat the oven to 375°F. Grease the insides of 2 pint-sized jars with non-stick cooking spray.
2. In a large skillet, cook the bacon over medium-high heat for a minute. Add the sausage meat and fry it until it is browned and cooked through. Make sure to break the meat up during the process. Allow the meat to cool down for 10 minutes.
3. In a medium bowl, whisk the eggs, milk, nutmeg, salt, and pepper.
4. Stir in the sweet potato, onion, and cooked meat.
5. Pour the egg mixture into the jars. Transfer the jars to a 9x9 baking dish.
6. Pour water into the baking dish until it covers the jars about half an inch up the sides.

7. Bake for 40-50 minutes, or until the eggs are set and the top has turned golden brown.
8. Let the casserole rest for 5 minutes before devouring it.

Nutritional Facts (372 g per single serving)
Calories 455
Fats 28 g
Carbs 10 g
Protein 41 g
Sodium 800 mg

Mini Cinnamon Rolls

Servings: 12

Ingredients
2 cups all-purpose flour
2 tablespoons granulated sugar
1 ¼ tablespoons baking powder
¾ teaspoons salt
¼ cup butter, cubed
¾ cup buttermilk

Filling:
¼ cup butter, melted
1 cup brown sugar
1 tablespoon cinnamon

Frosting:
2 cups powdered sugar
2-3 drops vanilla extract
Milk

Preparation
1. Preheat the oven to 350°F. Grease 12 half-pint jars with cooking spray.
2. In a large bowl, whisk together the flour, sugar, baking powder, and salt. Add the ¼ cup of butter cubes and rub it into the dry ingredients using your finger tips to create a coarse cornmeal texture.
3. Pour in the buttermilk in 2-3 batches, making sure to completely incorporate the liquid each time. You should end up with a smooth dough.

4. Tip the dough out onto a lightly floured surface and knead for about 5 minutes. Roll the dough out to from a rectangular shape, ¼ inch thick.
5. In a small bowl, whisk together the melted butter, brown sugar, and cinnamon. Spread the paste all over the dough.
6. Roll the dough lengthwise, turning it away from you. Cut the roll evenly into 12 pieces. Transfer each piece into a half-pint canning jar.
7. Bake for 15-20 minutes or until the dough is completely cooked through. Set it aside and allow it to cool completely.
8. Meanwhile, make the frosting. Put the powdered sugar into a small bowl. Stir in just enough milk for all the sugar to dissolve. Dribble in 2-3 drops of vanilla extract. Drizzle the frosting on top of the cinnamon rolls. Enjoy them as is, or cover with lids and keep them in the fridge for up to a week.

Nutritional Facts (75 g per single serving)
Calories 266
Fats 5 g
Carbs 46 g
Protein 3 g
Sodium 25 mg

Baked Blueberry Oatmeal

Servings: 6

Ingredients
1 ½ cups rolled oats
½ cup toasted pecans, chopped
1 ½ cups blueberries
1 ½ cups apple juice
1 large egg, lightly beaten
2 tablespoons honey
1 teaspoon ground cinnamon
¼ teaspoon salt

Preparation
1. Preheat the oven to 350°F.
2. In a small bowl, whisk together the oats, pecans, and blueberries. Portion the blueberry mixture evenly among 6 half-pint jars.
3. In another bowl, mix together the apple juice, egg, honey, cinnamon, and salt.
4. Pour the wet ingredients into the jars.
5. Bake for 25-30 minutes, or until the oats turn golden brown.
6. Allow them to cool down slightly before enjoying them warm.

Nutritional Facts (163 g per single serving)
Calories 297
Fats 10 g
Carbs 45 g
Protein 8 g
Sodium 16 mg

Muesli Oats with Pistachio and Figs

Servings: 2

Ingredients
1 cup rolled oats
1 cup orange juice, freshly squeezed
1 tablespoon honey
2 tablespoons plain yogurt
¼ cup pistachios, roasted
6 plums, deseeded and roughly sliced
1 fig, sliced into wedges

Preparation
1. In 2 pint-sized jars, soak the oats in orange juice overnight in the refrigerator.
2. The next day, mix the honey and yogurt into the oats. Finish off with the fruits and nuts. Serve immediately.

Nutritional Facts (467 g per single serving)
Calories 602
Fats 14 g
Carbs 106 g
Protein 20 g
Sodium 9 mg

Conclusion

Mornings are busy, but there is no need to compromise on a nutritious breakfast. With a few minutes' preparation, everyone can have a warm (or cold), tasty, healthy meal to start their day. The recipes in this book are easy enough that children can choose and prepare their own canning jar breakfasts, and this will give you a chance to let them feel independent, while you teach them about healthy eating.

We hope you enjoy these recipes, and use them as a starting point to go ahead and prepare your own omelets, muffins, pancakes, smoothies, and yogurt parfait breakfasts! With canning jars, the possibilities are endless.

About the Author

Louise Davidson is an avid cook who likes simple flavors and easy-to-make meals. She lives in Tennessee with her husband, her three grown children, her two dogs, and the family's cat, Whiskers. She loves the outdoor and has mastered the art of camp cooking on open fires and barbecue grills.

In colder months, she loves to whip up some slow cooker meals, and uses her favorite cooking tools in her kitchen, the cast iron pans, and Dutch oven. She also is very busy preparing Christmas treats for her extended family and friends. She gets busy baking for the holiday season sometimes as early as October. Her recipes are cherished by everyone who has tasted her foods and holiday treats.

Louise is a part-time writer of cookbooks, sharing her love of food, her experience, and her family's secret recipes with her readers.

She also loves to learn and share tips and tricks to make life a breeze.

More Books from Louise Davidson

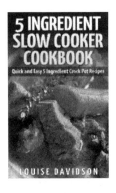  

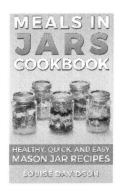

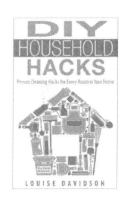

CAMPING
COOKBOOK
FOIL PACKET
RECIPES
LOUISE DAVIDSON

CAMPING
COOKBOOK
DUTCH OVEN
CAST IRON RECIPES
LOUISE DAVIDSON

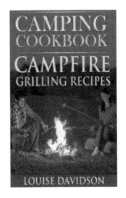

CAMPING
COOKBOOK
CAMPFIRE
GRILLING RECIPES
LOUISE DAVIDSON

CAMPING
COOKBOOK
Fun, Quick and Easy Campfire Recipes
LOUISE DAVIDSON

HOLIDAY
Baking
Favorite Quick and Easy
Sweet Treat Recipes
LOUISE DAVIDSON

HOLIDAY
BAKING
Easy Sweet Treat Recipes
LOUISE DAVIDSON

Easy Homemade Holiday Gifts
Louise Davidson

ULTIMATE
Holiday Party
Finger Food &
Drink Recipes
Louise Davidson

Thanksgiving
Cookbook
Louise Davidson

Appendix - Cooking Conversion Charts

1. Volumes

US Fluid Oz.	US	US Dry Oz.	Metric Liquid ml
¼ oz.	2 tsp.	1 oz.	10 ml.
½ oz.	1 tbsp.	2 oz.	15 ml.
1 oz.	2 tbsp.	3 oz.	30 ml.
2 oz.	¼ cup	3½ oz.	60 ml.
4 oz.	½ cup	4 oz.	125 ml.
6 oz.	¾ cup	6 oz.	175 ml.
8 oz.	1 cup	8 oz.	250 ml.

Tsp.= teaspoon - tbsp.= tablespoon – oz.= ounce – ml.= millimeter

2. Oven Temperatures

Celsius (°C)	Fahrenheit (°F)
90	220
110	225
120	250
140	275
150	300
160	325
180	350
190	375
200	400
215	425
230	450
250	475
260	500

59206731R00046

Made in the USA
Lexington, KY
29 December 2016